The Golden Triangle and Japan

Glenn Myers

Authentic
LIFESTYLE

First published 2005 by Authentic Lifestyle

Authentic Lifestyle is an imprint of Authentic Media
9 Holdom Avenue, Bletchley, Milton Keynes MK1 1QR, UK
and PO Box 1047, Waynesboro, GA 30830-2047 USA

11 10 09 08 07 06 05   7 6 5 4 3 2 1

British Library Cataloguing in Publication Data
A catalogue record for this book is available from the British Library

ISBN 1-85078-610-0

This book is produced by Wellspring Media, the UK media department of WEC International.

WEC is an international, interdenominational missions agency aiming to bring the Christian gospel
to the remaining unevangelized nations of the world. WEC currently has over 1700 workers from
nearly 50 nations serving Christ together in around 60 countries.

www.wec-int.org
www.wec-int.org.uk

Designed by Christopher Lawther, Teamwork, Lancing, West Sussex.
Cover design by Adrian Searle and Sam Richardson.
Typeset by Profile PPS Ltd, Rewe, Exeter, Devon
and printed and bound in Great Britain by Printpoint, Bradford, W. Yorks.

CONTENTS

Start here

This *Briefing* looks at two completely different corners of the wider Buddhist world: Myanmar, Thailand and Cambodia, South East Asian countries on the banks of the Mekong River which share many cultural characteristics and for which we have borrowed the term, 'The Golden Triangle'; and Japan. Other *Briefings* have already looked at *China* and at the Muslim parts of South East Asia (*The Rim of Fire*).

My research assistant Chrissie visited Thailand and Myanmar and interviewed a number of people both there and in the UK, gathered information, and collected the photos. I'm very grateful for her hard work and creative suggestions throughout this project. The photos are copyright WEC International.

Thanks to all those who gave interviews and commented on drafts. Some of you gave up considerable amounts of your time. You know who you are: thank you all very much for your insights and patience. The book's failings are all mine, however.

I have tried to write as honestly and fairly as I can about Buddhism, folk religion and the issues that seem important in different nations, though inevitably as an outsider and in a very brief format. Insiders will see things differently. I recognize that nothing can replace first-hand encounters and discussions and I hope this book will promote that.

Thanks also to Cordelia and our children, our church supporters, my colleagues in WEC International, and my long-time and longsuffering editor, Jeremy Mudditt.

Glenn Myers, April 2005

FOLK RELIGION

The spiritual environment into which the Christian Church is trying to get established is dominated by folk religion in various forms and by Buddhism (considered on the following page). Folk religion is much more of a force here than it is in the West. In Japan, state Shintoism is the national cult. In Myanmar, Thailand and Cambodia making offerings and paying respects to spiritual beings sometimes called *nats* are widely seen as essential to a successful life, even in high government circles.

The names, regions of operation and influence of spirit powers are widely known and discussed. People put up spirit shrines with the same zeal that we in many parts of the West put up safety notices or fire certificates. People build careers in diagnosing, preventing and curing spiritual problems, or casting spells, or creating charms.

All this effort is an attempt to get on the right side of gods, demons, ghosts and ancestors, to avoid evil forces like bad luck or bad magic, and thus to promote good fortune, health, prosperity and healing. Its effect, of course, is to reverse the first commandment, that is, to have plenty of other gods rather than God.

A culture of spirit-appeasement raises two great challenges for the Church. The first is fully to take up the robust stance against unholy spirits that Jesus himself modelled. The second is to see the renewal of minds and of cultures, so that God is at the heart of life rather than the gods.

Pascal Khoo Thwe, a Catholic tribesman from Myanmar describes what results when this doesn't happen.

'My grandmother had her own way of reconciling the two faiths. She would kill a chicken, slitting its throat and offering its blood as a libation to the spirits of the farm after each Mass of thanksgiving. The priest told her that it was unnecessary to do that because the Mass had already pleased the highest God. But Grandma had her own reasons: "The gods are like government officials. If you want things done quickly, you have to bribe the small ones."'[1]

BUDDHISM

- Founded by Siddhartha Gautama, born around 563BC in North India.

- Buddhist scriptures spread over many thousands of pages and resemble theories of nuclear physics in their subtlety and other-worldliness.[2] The central problem is that to exist is to suffer. Though my experience of being an independent person is an illusion, it is one that repeatedly recurs through many rebirths. The solution to all this existence and suffering is detachment, that is, the extinction of all one's feelings. Once I am suitably detached and enlightened, I attain Nirvana, a reabsorption into oneness, the extinction of individual consciousness. Right living, thinking and meditating are deemed to be the route to Nirvana.

- Around the start of the Christian era, a new form of Buddhism called Mahayana Buddhism took shape. 'Mahayana' means 'big ferry' — the idea is that it carries lots of people across the river to Nirvana. Its followers dubbed the older, stricter Buddhism 'Theravada' ('little ferry').

- By the 7th century AD, the centre of Theravada Buddhism had moved to Sri Lanka. From here, it spread to the countries of the Golden Triangle.

- Meanwhile Mahayana Buddhism, which according to one author involves 'less discipline, less devotion, less direction, less demand, less despondency and despair'[3] spread to Bhutan, Nepal, Tibet, China, Mongolia, Northern Vietnam and in increasingly diffused forms, to Japan.

- Many other streams of Buddhist thought can be traced, such as Tibetan Buddhism, which borrows from the occult Hindu practices called Tantrism, and in which the Dalai Lama and the Panchen Lama are significant figures; and Zen Buddhism, with its strong focus on meditation and paradox. (Zen's symbol, a former Zen Buddhist told me, is an open circle, erased.)

- Western Buddhism has found a niche as a value system for people who care about peace and reconciliation, animal welfare, environmental issues, self-improvement, stress-reduction and alternative therapies, but who also prefer to live in a different spiritual environment from that defined by the Christian faith.

Buddhism's appeal is perhaps that it takes the world as it is without asking how or why it came to be. Then it offers ideas and techniques by which we might deal with the symptoms of suffering and pain, and improve our lives. Many of these therapies work at a certain level but without (Christians would argue) actually healing the root problem which is a self-centred rejection of a loving God.

Oddly, one of the attractions of Buddhism appears to be that it lowers expectation. You have zillions of lives in which to get things right. Asked what would happen when he finally reached enlightenment, Tenzin Gyatso, the Dalai Lama, replied, 'I am only a beginner. I don't know ... it will take several aeons ... There is no hurry.'[4]

– 1 –

Myanmar

Expect extremes: this is Asia. Myanmar is a large country — the size of France and the UK combined. The Himalayas crowd in from the north and spill down the eastern and western borders, fencing the country off from its neighbours. An enormous river, the Ayeyarwaddy or Irrawaddy bisects the whole country, and is bridged just once. It has giant countries (India and China) on its shoulders; and giant problems, magnified versions of Asia's problems, which have roosted in Myanmar like crows.

A pity: it's a beautiful land, where you can watch a farmer in a conical hat guiding a buffalo-pulled plough against a backdrop of snowy mountains; or see thousands of golden shrines in the former capital cities of ruined kingdoms; or climb jagged limestone hills that remind you of Chinese scroll paintings, overlooking misty lakes.

Myanmar is humid and fertile, half covered in forests. In the capital, Yangon, (whose name means 'end of strife') you can find the largest and oldest golden monument in the world, the 2,500-year-old Shwe Dagon pagoda. The jungles are full of life. Gems and jade are buried in the mountains. Beaches stretch out languidly against the Andaman Sea. Coral lies off the shore. It could be idyllic. It isn't.

Myanmar vies with Nepal, Bhutan, Laos and Timor-Leste to be the poorest country in Asia. Its health service was rated by the World Health Organization recently as 190th and worst in the world. It is ruled by people who devote (outsiders claim) 40% of the national wealth to defending themselves against their fellow-citizens but a mere 1% on health and education. There are thousands of displaced people in the jungles and the universities are shut most of the time in fear of student politics.

The country is a world-class exporter of drugs: the number two producer of heroin in the world, after Afghanistan. It is number one in methamphetamine ('speed' or 'ice' in the West), which needs no poppy fields, and of which Adolf Hitler had a daily fix. In 2001, Myanmar's jungle cookhouses produced 800 million tablets.

Given all this, few countries, perhaps, clamour more urgently for faith and prayer and holistic Christian involvement. What follows is a tentative attempt to outline some of the story.

Let's look at:

1. Nation
2. Church
3. Prospects

1. NATION

Indian traders brought Buddhism to Myanmar in the first few centuries AD. Unlike in the Mediterranean region, where the early Christian Church tried to displace the old idols, Burmese Buddhism merely passed through to the head of the pantheon and left all the original gods in their former jobs — a takeover but not a restructuring.

State-supported Buddhism subsequently led to Myanmar's finest days, the Pagan and later Ava Kingdoms, where temples were built and gold was lavished around in quantities reminiscent of Israel under King Solomon.

Two-thirds of the people of Myanmar (let's call them Burmese in deference to the country's former name) are Burman, that is, belonging to the dominant

Burmese-speaking ethnic group. As the Javanese dominate Indonesia, the Han Chinese dominate China, or the English dominate the UK, so Burman culture predominates in Myanmar.

The rest of the population belong to many different tribal groups. Myanmar's troubles are made worse because of the fractured relationships between the majority group and the minorities.

Myanmar was colonized late (1885) by the British and gained its freedom early (1948). According to some observers the British ran Myanmar in ways reminiscent of today's junta: they fielded many troops, burnt down whole 'rebel villages', mined the rubies to exhaustion, and controlled the trade in teak and crude oil.

Myanmar re-entered independent life as a country made up of seven Burman provinces and seven tribal states. It had no powerful and respected institutions from either its own independent traditions or from colonialism. After a brief and troubled democratic prelude, the Army took power in 1962, and, despite much constitutional window-dressing, there they have stayed. In its current form, the military government is called the State Peace and Development Council (SPDC), a name they adopted with advice from an American brand-management company.

MILITARY RULE

SPDC rule has been a disaster. The army has:

- Taken over the old industries, and run them incompetently and corruptly.
- Crushed political dissent and criticism.
- Repelled foreign investors.
- Made ludicrously bad decisions. For example, in 1987, U Ne Win who was

dictator from 1962 to 1988, cancelled all the existing currency and replaced it with notes denominated in 9s, his lucky number.

- Planted landmines, even to protect minor installations like electricity pylons.
- Conscripted children.
- Made many people work as forced labourers on infrastructure projects.
- Failed to provide enough schools and when tribal communities have started their own schools, sometimes shut them down.
- Shot, raped and burned their way through many villages belonging to ethnic minorities.

One might wonder what the SPDC is good at. 'They have built some good golf courses,' said one Burmese to a foreign journalist.[5] And they are good at sloganeering. Examples, pasted over the country, include, 'Anyone who is riotous, destructive or unruly is our enemy.' 'Observance of discipline leads to safety.'

With bullies at the top, corruption and oppression have had opportunity to spread through the whole country. In a visit in November 2002, the Christian human rights organization Christian Solidarity International gave an example of army behaviour. A man was encouraged by the government to develop a fish farm. It succeeded, so the SPDC took it over and demanded that the man paid a huge amount for a licence so that he could have his job back.[6]

Teachers give paid tuition in the evenings to the same children whom they should have taught during the day. Hospital doctors run private clinics that charge 'test fees'. Once you've paid your 'test fees' to the doctor, he smoothes the way into the state hospital. Want a form from a government office? Certainly — but perhaps you'd like to buy our calendar first. In trouble with the state security forces? Try a small contribution. Want your mail delivered? Give the mail-carrier some regular 'tea money'.

The 'Golden Land' — so fertile and rich — suffers food shortages, power shortages and criminally denies large numbers of people basic necessities like clean water and good sanitation. There may be a million people with HIV. Drug addiction is rampant. Conditions are worst in the ethnic states. The root cause, of course, is a deeper shortage — a shortage of justice and righteousness.

PROTESTS

This has not gone unprotested. During all Myanmar's time as an independent country, the tribal regions have been fighting with the centre. All sides have been accused of recruiting child soldiers, raising money through the drug trade, and mass killings.

For their treatment of ethnic minorities, the SPDC is condemned by the UN, the US, the EU and even Japan. (Myanmar's fellow members of the Association of South East Asian Nations — ASEAN — tend to be more circumspect.) Many countries refuse to trade with Myanmar and charities can have prickly relations. This may be a righteous response: unfortunately the short-term result is yet more suffering for the poor.

A bigger headache for the government has been the protests of the Burmese people. A peaceful uprising that began on the auspicious date of 8/8/1988 led to murderous repression — Myanmar's Tiananmen — which led in turn to the military government being rattled into calling elections for 1990. Much to their shock, the army-related party received fewer than ten seats in the parliament, while 85% of the vote went to the recently formed National League for Democracy. This party was headed by Daw Aung San Suu Kyi, the daughter of the greatest of the independence leaders.

As is now well-known, the army annulled the 1990 elections and have spent the intervening years harassing, arresting, and imprisoning members of the National League for Democracy. Aung San Suu Kyi was awarded the Nobel Peace Prize. Her steadfast, principled opposition to the government has won universal respect and something close to adoration in Myanmar itself. When Burmese talk about the 'The Lady', they only have one person in mind.

All this has driven the SPDC to behave something like an addict lying to counsellors about trying to give up the habit. They are under enormous international pressure to reform their ways, and they try to show willing, but soon are back injecting themselves. Aung San Suu Kyi is released from house arrest ... then disappears again ... they open negotiations with her ... then close them ... they are near to sharing power with ethnic groups ... but now they are undermining them again. When it comes to seizing power and crushing people, the Army just can't kick the habit.

They are forever reforming the constitution, but never quite getting around to putting it to a vote. In 1994 trade minister Lieutenant General Tun Kyi told journalists, 'When the constitution is completed, democracy will be restored.' Ten years later, the talk was much the same.[7]

2. CHURCH

The first encounters between Myanmar and the Christian faith are lost, but probably took place through the pioneering efforts of the Assyrian Church of the East, perhaps somewhere in the second half of the first millennium. Stone crosses in central Myanmar from the 12th century are the earliest archaeological evidence of a Christian presence. They may have originated with an invading army that contained Syrians or Armenians — a whisper of a Christian story that is today largely lost. In 1503 a Frenchman travelling in Asia heard reports of churches both in Myanmar and Thailand.

Memories of Christian encounters may have been carried through the generations in the folk traditions of the hill peoples. As we shall see in a moment, many peoples held onto traditions of 'a book about the one true God' that had been lost but would be brought again by pale-faced people from overseas.

With the opening of the sea routes between Europe and Asia, Catholic missions eventually arrived (1722). But it was the Protestants, and especially the Baptists, who came to shape the Burmese Christian scene most profoundly, and that through the huge pioneering figure of Adoniram Judson.

Judson and his wife Ann have the distinction of being just about the first overseas, cross-cultural missionaries of the United States. Their ship docked in Yangon in July 1813. They weren't especially successful if what they came to do was start churches. Nor were they the popular stereotype of the nineteenth century missionary, if that is of the lordly spiritual sidekick to Western empire builders. They experienced profound powerlessness, indifference or opposition from colonial powers, rejection and contempt from the Burmese. They suffered jail, bereavement, destitution, despair, lack of visible success, illness, and profound, ministry-sapping depression. Yet Myanmar is today still being shaken and shaped because they got off the boat, and bore their witness to Jesus.

THE WHITE MAN WITH THE BOOK

One day, a rough, lanky man named Ko Thah-Byu appeared at Judson's door, seeking work. Judson recognized him as a Karen, one of the hill tribes. He had seen Karen in the market-places but kept his focus steadily on the Burman people. Judson found Ko Thah-Byu some employment.

Judson and other members of his household shared the gospel with Ko Thah-Byu without much response at first. But then something changed. Ko Thah-Byu began asking questions. He learnt to read, and started to study the portions of the Burmese Bible that Judson had translated.

When two new missionaries, George and Sarah Boardman, moved south-west to start work in the town of Tavoy, Ko Thah-Byu asked to come along. They agreed and baptised him. Ko Thah-Byu used the new location as a convenient base to start visiting his fellow tribespeople.

Ko Thah-Byu then began revealing a gifting and anointing that took his church-starting achievements far beyond anything the missionaries were capable of. He entered village after village in the hills and preached — and hundreds responded. The further he travelled, the more he preached, and the more he preached, the more whole villages turned to Christ.

Before long, other villagers were themselves passing on the message and something like a spiritual avalanche was building momentum among the 800,000 Karen. Some more American missionaries arrived in a town 300 miles northwest of Tavoy, and found 5,000 Karen already waiting to be baptized, the hard work of winning them to Jesus already done. What was happening was one of the first 'people movements' in the history of Protestant missions. While Judson was winning Burmans one-by-one on the plains, in the hills, the Karen were coming family-by-family and village-by-village.

What was Ko Thah-Byu preaching? It turned out that the Karen had treasured folk memories of a high, eternal, loving god called Y'wa. (Had they learnt this from the Assyrian missionaries of a thousand years before? Who knows?) Their sins, they taught, had driven them away from Y'wa. But Y'wa had not forgotten them. One day a 'white foreigner' was to arrive from across the sea with wings (or sails) and bring Y'wa's white book (some had it as a golden book) that would tell them how to return to Y'wa. Ko Thah-Byu was saying in effect, 'The time has come! And here's the book!' And thousands of Karen were concluding, 'That's right'.

That wasn't the end. The gospel jumped across to other hill tribes. The Kachin, half a million of them, who also believed in a high, hidden, good God and a lost book. The Lahu, a quarter of a million of them, who had storytellers who kept the message alive about their high god Gui'Sha. If you set out with ten armloads of walking sticks, and walked until each one was worn down, you still wouldn't find Gui'Sha, they said. But when the right time comes, a white brother will come with a white book, bringing the laws of Gui'Sha. One day a white-faced missionary called William Marcus Young was spotted by some Lahu preaching from his white-paged Bible in a market place (he was trying to bring the gospel to a completely different tribe). The Lahu headhunted him, as it were, and from 1904 until his death in 1936, Young saw more than 2,000 Lahu each year get baptized.[8]

So Myanmar's church history progressed: rapid, collective turnings to Christianity among many of the hill tribes, slow, painful, against-the-grain conversations among the peoples of the plains. That is still the pattern today. Among 31 million plains-dwelling Bamar (Burman), you can count just 30,000 Christians.[9]

THE CHURCH TODAY

Churches that grow up among impoverished tribespeople who are on the wrong end of brutal and repressive dictatorship will have many contradictory things true of them: zeal and nominalism, light and darkness. Nor are all the different tribes' experiences of the Christian faith the same. The mixture takes some unpacking.

POVERTY AND PRESTIGE

When you are extremely poor, and you hear that Christians overseas are wallowing in money like hippos in mud, it's hard for this not to distort your practice of Christianity. Here are some of the consequences.

- Tribal churches are Baptist, Assemblies of God and Anglican, among others, and they usually have a 19th-century Western look-and-feel. Churchly goings-on in Myanmar are typically formal, minister-led, and prestigious. There may be robes, a choir, two offerings (first the tithe, then the free-will offering), a long pastoral prayer, a long sermon. Nothing wrong in this perhaps, except the fear that the flowing robes, the lofty status of the minister, and the lack of other outlets for the ambitious man, may attract exactly the wrong sort of candidate as spiritual leader.

- Too much emphasis can be made on the pomp, too little on the internals. Myanmar's Christian movement has great strengths, as we shall see below, but a tradition of lay discipleship, grounded in personal devotion to scripture and prayer, isn't as common as you'd wish.

- In the capital, many pastors run their own little Bible schools. There is much needless duplication. And often the teaching is in English, which is more prestigious than practical.

- Many of the older established Bible colleges have largely sold out to a liberal, Western theological stance that, whatever its virtues may be, does not seem to have much life-changing power in East or West.

- If you, as a foreign Christian,

visit a Burmese church, you might well be asked to preach. The real reason for the invitation comes afterwards, when the pastor hands over a list of suitable projects for foreign sponsorship. And some of the sponsored projects are almost a parody of Christian care. Witness, for example, the luxury 'orphanage', its roomy accommodation half empty, peopled with children whose parents were rich enough to bribe the staff to get them in.

GUNS AND DRUGS

Then add severe political oppression to the poverty and powerlessness. This too strains and distorts the Church.

Civil war. The tribal groups have offered the most stubborn and bloody resistance to the SPDC, and the tribal groups are home to nearly all the Christians. Inevitably the Church is severely scarred and restricted by this conflict.

Large tribal Christian conventions have sometimes been banned. It's hard to get permission to renovate an old church building or put up a new one. Christian monuments like the huge concrete crosses favoured by the Chin people have been torn down. Pagodas have been constructed instead. Pastors have been thrown in jail.

Some tribal groups, particularly the Karen, are involved in a civil war with the Burmese army. The sufferings of these people, many of them keen Christians, is hard to imagine: whole communities violently forced from their homes, shelled, bombed and harried in the jungle, their children dying all around for lack of medical care. People who have visited from outside are amazed at the tenacity, goodness and faith of some of these people.

The terrible paradox of living a Christian life while being part of an armed terrorist insurgency against an unjust government is lived out in full today in the jungles of Myanmar. Fewer than half the Karen profess Christianity, but the Christian minority are seemingly caught up in the war along with the majority who still follow traditional tribal beliefs. It's a fight for life; yet it's also a grisly insurgency involving landmines and child soldiers, funded by drugs and illegal logging.

One enthusiastic foreign visitor reported it this way: 'If you met the Karen soldiers (who wear flip-flops and are all unpaid refugees) your faith would increase — they *pray* everytime they defend their villages. Currently there are 54,000 Burmese SPDC [Army] against them — with just 1,500 of them along a very long border area. But, they say, "with God we can achieve anything. We are fighting for righteousness."' Some Christian-inspired groups from the United States have no problems with any of this and are raising money for them and (who knows) probably supplying weapons and expertise too.

Bribery and corruption. The shortage of righteousness and justice makes it genuinely hard for anyone to live in Myanmar without resorting to bribery and corruption. Some would say it's impossible. Do Christians (local or foreign) pay bribes? Some do. Some don't: and suffer for it.

Drugs, trafficking, and deforestation. Evil begets evil and Northern Myanmar buzzes with many of the evils that are particularly fashionable to decry in the West just now: drug smuggling, environmental devastation, and the trafficking of young girls into the sex trade. Are there people who attend churches on Sunday and traffic drugs or young girls during the rest of the week? Sadly there are — testimony to the evils of nominal Christianity and to the need for Biblical teaching.

AN OPPOSITE SPIRIT

It's a happier task to report on the Church's strengths, and the ways, despite great poverty and restriction, it demonstrates an opposite spirit to all the brutality, tribalism and corruption.

The best of the tribal churches are ardently evangelistic, winning their own people to Christ, and sending hundreds of indigenous missionaries on mountain trails to bring the gospel to other tribes and cultures within Myanmar and beyond. The Karen, for example, are approaching 50% Christian. The Church as a whole appears to be growing, from just over 6% of the population in 1991 to approaching 9% by 2001.[10]

Some of the Christians are starting churches in the cities, based round the Burmese language rather than their tribal one. Such churches can grow to be multi-ethnic congregations. This is, surely, the start of a new story of Burmans and tribals mingling in the cities, with the gospel making bridges from one to the other.

A number of people from the tribal churches have fought hard to get an education and are in positions of responsibility all over Myanmar. It's easy to forget that within the government there are many believers acting as salt and light, making Myanmar a better place.

Then, tribal Christianity at its best can create a quality of Christian community many of us from more individualistic traditions hardly glimpse. Here's an eyewitness account of life among Chin tribespeople, that could be repeated widely among the Karen and Lisu and others.

> *The sense of family and community is everywhere; the young are respectful of their elders, children obey their parents long into adulthood. Grandparents, now old and frail, spend long hours in prayer, secure in the care of their loved ones. Family members pool resources to travel for education or work.*
>
> *Everywhere churches abound ... Every shop, every restaurant seems to be Christian owned ... bicycles outnumber all other vehicles on the roads ... Electricity is variable, street lighting non-existent. But the people of God have a vision to care for the poor of their community.*

This same regular Western visitor described to us one couple running an orphanage for forty destitute children; a doctor charging 5p per consultation for about 100 patients a day; a businessman opening a secondary boarding school — opposite instances to the graft and oppression that you can find elsewhere.

She said of the secondary boarding school: 'Here there is no lack of commitment; the students appreciate the compulsory 8 to 11pm study period, many take up the optional additional hour till midnight. Their agenda includes twice-daily worship, an amazing experience for the visitor: three hundred and fifty radiant young faces, worshipping, praying more fervently than most adults, reading the scriptures in unison, listening with rapt attention.'

There are rural Bible schools who with antiquated resources and severe limits on the curriculum are training and discipling young people and seeking to better the communities around them. I know of hospital visitation teams who give their own money and donate their own blood to keep patients alive and well. Christians, as ever in this region, care for the lepers, and run orphanages and clinics.

3. PROSPECTS

The military's grip, in common with many dictatorships, is harsh but somewhat uncertain. They almost lost control in 1988 and again in 1990. Disagreements occasionally surface between the leaders. It is probably fair to say that the military do not actually know what they want for Myanmar, beyond the continuation of their own rule.

Meanwhile, they are feeling a squeeze from many directions. In politics, the 'bad cop' routine of the West shames and isolates Myanmar. The Association of South East Asian Nations plays 'good cop', inviting the generals, for example, to chair the ASEAN meetings in 2006. I suspect the military would prefer it if outsiders just left them alone to brutalize their citizens in peace. It was interesting to see a recent article on the government-sponsored website *myanmar.com* insisting how well the government was treating the Catholics and other 'Christian sects'. Whether or not they were telling the truth, they were clearly sore at all the criticism they'd been getting — a fact to encourage those dogged protesters who stand outside Burmese embassies with hand-made placards on cold winter's days.

Nor can the military keep out the seeping influence of materialism which in ways both good and bad builds up pressure for change. Slowly, the government is having to open up the country for trade. Business opportunities are growing and being taken up by Chinese, other Asian, and Western expatriates — some of whom are Christians. Visas are getting easier to obtain. Censorship of all kinds is becoming less heavy, driven by the needs to attract business. The press is becoming slightly more free, urban society much more free. Materialism seeps into the tribal areas, and people see the erosion of the former values (both good and bad) and know that soon, things must change.

TIPPING THE SCALES

Myanmar is inevitably ripening towards a new day. How can we Christians help hurry and shape that process? Here are some areas of opportunity.

A new openness to Christian witness. There is a surprising openness to the Christian faith among some of Myanmar's Buddhist monks. Some are studying the Bible. Christian radio broadcasters receive mail inquiries from them. Visitors find them receptive to the gospel. Even though it's very hard to 'come out' as a Christian, some monks have done so. If they started to do this in any numbers, we would be witnessing a new day for the Christian faith in Myanmar.

More generally, the Burmese people are warm, welcoming and generous in their appreciation of visitors. One tourist reported:

> [A friend and I were] sitting in a public square around lunchtime writing postcards … Some of the students of the private classes came up to us to practice. Then at around 1pm or 1:30pm they would ask if we were willing to go with them to their classes. Apparently they are asked by their teachers to take a tourist to use as pronunciation and listening practice. We nicknamed the practice 'nab a tourist'. The teachers are university graduates whose pronunciation is picked up from the radio. The class is sometimes up to 100 students all crowded into one small room on benches … They are full of monks who often are allowed to go in free.

Political change. No government can completely foul up a country and stay in power forever. The SPDC must fall or drastically change at some point. The real questions are when and how.

James Mawdsley speaks with more authority than most outsiders on the business of confronting Myanmar's generals, and perhaps gives us Christians some pointers to prayer. An English Catholic, he entered Myanmar several times during the late 1990s to make human rights protests and face certain imprisonment. (He experienced significant spiritual renewal during one of his spells in prison.) His diary recorded why he kept going back:

> I do not have to keep returning to Burma indefinitely. But there is something I must do before I can turn my attention to a less direct approach — I have to voice the truth without fear. This is something I have not yet done, and until I do it I cannot settle in England. And the truth is simple: that the SPDC hold their control over Burma only by violence and engendering fear.[11]

For Mawdsley, the real battle was with fear. A Church that is peace-loving, multi-ethnic and fearless could have an immense influence for good on the future shape of Myanmar.

Networking. Some observers talk of younger leaders who are beginning to reshape and renew the Church through a commitment to networking, partnership, and servant leadership — this is a new kind of Burmese Christian leadership, one urgently needed.

Foreigners may have a part to play too. The last missionaries were forced out of Myanmar in 1965. But now, business, non-governmental organizations and the education sector all offer opportunities for foreign Christians to serve in Myanmar, not as religious workers but simply by their own lives, integrity and friendships, as partners in the Christian community.

In addition, local and international mission groups are trying to find ways to bring the gospel to the whole of Myanmar in word and deed — translating the Bible and distributing literature, for example, or producing radio programmes, or showing the *Jesus* film. Holistic development aid is now possible in some of the tribal areas. Leadership training is another key area of opportunity, opening the way to a further strengthening and renewing of the Church. The Christians used to run all the best schools until the government nationalized them in 1964. Perhaps the Christian influence in education could rise again. Sensitive partnership with existing churches is the key, and the great opportunity.

– 2 –

Thailand

BIRTHPANGS

If you could chose to be born in one of the countries of our 'Golden Triangle', you'd probably choose Thailand.

The calm-ish heart of a troubled region, it has not suffered the brutalities of Myanmar, nor the wars of Laos and Vietnam, nor the apocalypse of Cambodia. Even its many military coups have been, with a few bloody exceptions, mild by the standards of the region. Thailand's problems have more often arisen from being too welcoming to outsiders, and too easy-going.

That makes recent events all the more shocking and somehow, non-Thai. An insurgency inspired by Al-Qaeda has drawn Thai security forces into a savage conflict with some of the Muslims of the southern provinces. The Indian Ocean tsunami of December 26 2004 swept away five-and-half thousand people in a few seconds, half of them Thai, half of them visitors, the paradise-white beaches suddenly overwhelmed in walls of water and mud. Media reports for weeks afterwards in Thailand spoke of the empty resorts haunted by the ghostly sounds of tourists at play.

Avian flu and high-profile terror attacks are among further concerns that could shake the nation profoundly.

In politics, the Thai people have elected a more forceful and focussed government than has been seen for years. This administration is hustling Thailand along a familiar Asian path, but one that's relatively new to Thailand: rapid economic development and social reform, alongside (claims of) loss of media freedom and of abuses of human rights. Government action against illegal drugs is perhaps characteristic of the new political tempo: a drastic cleanup, hundreds dead.

At the same time, in a completely different area of Thai affairs, the Christian Church, long accustomed to slow growth and cultural isolation, is showing in places a growing confidence, momentum and faith.

THE STORY SO FAR

Thai history is like a reverse image of Burmese or Cambodian history, a gain for one being a loss to another. When the Thai moved to Thailand, they usurped the Khmer. When the Khmer Empire in Cambodia fell, the builders of Cambodia's Angkor Wat moved over to adorn Thailand's Ayutthaya with their astonishing architecture. Ayutthaya was eventually destroyed by the Burmese and a new royal Thai dynasty was established in Bangkok ... and so on.

Near the end of the Ayutthaya era, Roman Catholic missionaries had an impact on the Thai royal family. For a time the designated heir-apparent was a Catholic. But after the king died in 1688 a palace coup ended the life of the heir, and turned Thailand in on itself for over a century.

Three great Buddhist kings then shaped the Thai story.

Rama IV (also known as Mongkut) (r.1851-1868) had been a Buddhist monk for 27 years. Along with his successor Rama V (Chulalongkorn) (1868-1910), he managed the remarkable trick of modernizing Thailand, avoiding colonization, and strengthening the national identity around the ideas of Nation, Religion, and King, the three parallel stripes in the Thai flag. The anniversary of King Chulalongkorn's death is still a national holiday, notable for the sight of students and civil servants stretching out flat before his statue on Rajdamnoen Nok Avenue.

The third remarkable king is the current one, Rama IX (Bhumipol). He was enthroned in 1950, and has been a force for honesty and stability in an era that (since a military coup in 1932) has seen 17 coups, 53 governments and 16 new constitutions. The Thai revere their monarch and see him as a symbol and guardian of all that is good about their land. Among many other things, he has overseen a steady increase in health and wealth, maintained political stability, and been a notable champion of religious freedom.

MISSIONS

Thailand is an hospitable country to Christian missionaries. Early Protestant missionaries to Thailand were focussed on the Chinese. The first Chinese Protestant church in all Asia was started in Bangkok in 1837 by a Baptist missionary called William Dean — and is still worshipping today.

The early Protestant missionaries to Thailand worked diligently and at great personal cost. Many died young. As well as preaching the gospel, they built schools and hospitals. They introduced printing, and were the main conduit by which Western medicine and modern science reached the country. They pioneered care for people with leprosy, setting the highest standards. The McKean leprosarium, for example, just south of Chiang Mai, opened in 1908 and was planted with every possible tropical fruit and flower to become a much sought-out haven. The missionaries planted, however, relatively few churches.

King Rama IV became a friend of some of the missionaries. They taught him both the gospel and English. But like many Thai he couldn't see the point of the gospel. He is said to have told the missionaries, 'What you teach [the people] to do is admirable, but what you teach them to believe is foolish.'[12]

By the beginning of the twentieth century numbers in the Thai Church were slowly rising, but this growth tailed away as theological liberalism took hold of large parts of the Church.

A SECOND TRY

After the Second World War, a new generation of young missionaries entered Thailand in conditions of great sacrifice. Take the first team of WEC missionaries, as typical of several groups. Arriving in 1947, they settled in remote western provinces. They had no privacy, plumbing, phones, electricity, fridges, fans, motorized transport, doctors, hospitals, or even a short-wave radio.

Once they had learned some language they became used to a familiar refrain, 'Buddhism and Christianity are the same!' Though a number of their friends dabbled in the Christian faith, few stuck with it — even when the power of God was remarkably present.

One time they were called to pray for a Thai man in a coma. In the room around him, his female relatives were preparing the flowers for his burial. Below the stilted house they could hear his male relatives putting together teak boards for his coffin. The leader of the WEC group asked for all the charms and spirit bracelets to be removed, laid his hand on the man's head, and prayed. The man opened his eyes. Over the next few months he returned to full health. He and his family joined the Christians; but even they struggled to stay the distance.

Others from this pioneering WEC team started clinics for lepers. They came with revolutionary new drugs and brought a standard of nursing and Christian care never before seen in the area. One of them explained the response:

> We explained the Gospel in simple words. But most of the patients seemed to want only the medicine we had to dispense and not our teaching. Only a few of the most badly diseased seemed interested in our message. Their families would have liked for us to take care of them altogether, as their disease brought shame to the family.[13]

THE CHURCHES THEY STARTED

Such was the story of all the missions in Thailand. Sow the gospel widely. Dig everything you know into the soil: prayer, sacrifice, signs, wonders, holistic health care. Some missionaries identified so closely with the Thai leprosy sufferers that they caught leprosy from them.

But then watch a meagre harvest spring up and watch even some of that wilt and fail. In Thailand you may sow, but you do not yet reap thirty-, sixty-, or a hundred-fold.

The only exception was among the tribal peoples, just like in Myanmar. The tribals make up less than five percent of the Thai population, but some of them such as the Lahu and the Karen have embraced the gospel and seen it change their communities.[14] Bible colleges that serve the ethnic minorities in Thailand are full; and in some regions, every tribal village has a church.[15]

TAKING IT SLOW

Many reasons for the slow growth of the Church among the Thai could be suggested. Buddhism's traditional place in national life and patriotism is one. A Christian worker put words in the mouth of an imaginary Bangkok resident, as a way of summarizing remarks he had heard many times over — and which perhaps go to the heart of the issue:

> We all feel that to be truly Thai, you have to be a Buddhist — that's what we were born into and brought up in. We all have shrines in our homes and many amulets to give us help in our daily lives. It's true we enjoy your western technology, but for Thai people, Buddhism is the religion of the heart, and that's how we wish it to remain! [16]

Another key reason might be the characteristic Thai lack of urgency about life. The *farang* (foreigner), 'carries his worries around like a dog carries fleas'.[17] The Thai Buddhist, in contrast, has many lifetimes to get things right, so why worry? Perhaps it is fair to characterize Thai people as being somewhere between relaxed and resigned when it comes to the big questions of life.

PROSPECTS

Which might seem to be the whole story, were it not for the endless pressure of rapid change. Nothing is standing still in Thailand. And tsunamis and insurgents apart, the big story is the fundamental restructuring and reordering of the nation, rural to urban, rice-paddy to factory, peasant to citizen. No-one knows where all this will end, or what further upheaval it will yet cause. But attitudes are changing.

The new government — civilian, stable and democratically elected — is itself a consequence of decades of rapid economic growth. So is its reforming agenda. Many of the things Thailand has been infamous for — the sex trade, HIV, drug addiction, corruption — are having war made on them, to the surprise of many in the country.

Prostitutes have been on the streets demonstrating against the cleaning up of Bangkok's so-called 'nightlife'. Tourist websites bewail the decline of cheap sex. One man recently was arrested and charged with owning six brothels. He was furious, not because it wasn't true, but because he had bribed the police a lot of money to keep quiet and they were breaking their side of the bargain.[18] Corruption in Buddhist temples is being exposed by the media.

Another highly important sign of wealth redistributing power is changing attitudes to the family. 'No, I don't want to see my extended family', the Bangkok resident might tell you. 'They only want a loan, and I won't see the money again.' Money, not family, is the new social insurance.

THE OPPORTUNITY

Not every generation sees upheaval like this. Which means the Christian Church — carefully and painstakingly established over the decades — now has an unusual opportunity.

Measured at its very widest the Church today has upwards of 800,000 people among Thailand's 64 millions.[19] Most congregations are small. Many aren't growing: little pockets of elderly people.

It's easy to become quite discouraged. One missionary observer wrote: 'The familiar scenarios' for Thai church leaders, 'include slow church growth after a hard slog, economic constriction, attractive job offers from other organizations, intractable church elders, a slump in offerings, lack of human skills for the job and physical, ethnic or marital stress.'

Yet there are clear signs of fresh things happening, hints that the Church may yet have the vigour, the confidence and the faith to rise to the challenges all around it.

The long tradition of Christ-centred social work is still strong, and has stayed relevant as Thai society has changed. World Vision's work among women and girls in Northern Thailand is aimed at (negatively) preventing them ever being procured for the flesh trade and (positively) helping them find education, skills, and self-worth. In Bangkok, local NGOs like Rahab Ministries are serving the bar-girls. They and other groups are also involved in advocacy and campaigning. The Christian groups are one of the reasons the child-sex trade in Thailand is (probably) beginning to decline.[20]

Some Christian leaders are being invited to teach in schools, a sign that Christian values are being seen as both distinct and perhaps freshly relevant within Thai society. This is a big change.

Some church leaders will claim anecdotally they are baptising more people than they used to — one or two per month, rather than one or two per year. New churches may be being started at a faster rate than previously.

Among some pastors and leaders there is observable what someone called 'a new sense of desperation in the Christians' prayers'.[21] It isn't entirely unknown for church leaders to be going on 40-day fasts.[22]

Prayer networks between churches are being woven together, signs of a growing vision for transforming whole regions through united prayer.

There are mega-churches in Bangkok these days. Other urban congregations are also too influential to be ignored as some minor ghetto phenomenon. A number of prominent celebrities have publicly turned to Christ.

In what turned out to be the few weeks before the tsunami, a US missions foundation funded a major campaign to offer a free copy of a book called 'Power for Living' to the whole of Thailand. As well as presenting the gospel, the book included testimonies from Thai celebrities. Adverts for the book appeared in magazines, on bus-stops and sky-train stations, and even on national TV. More than 400,000 copies were distributed and, more importantly, the Church reached a new mark in terms of its public exposure and, perhaps, its confidence and faith.

Umbrella organizations such as the Evangelical Fellowship of Thailand and the Churches of Christ in Thailand give the Christian movement a national, and somewhat united profile. The CCT was supplying food, water and cooking materials to tsunami victims within 48 hours of the disaster.

It's possible to overstate all of this. We aren't yet talking of rapid church growth such as might be observed in China, or even the openness to the gospel that can be found in Cambodia or Vietnam. Green shoots aren't the same as a harvest. But still, they're coming up.

- 3 -

Cambodia

Cambodia and its majority people the Khmer are famous for two things: *Angkor* and *Angkar*.

ANGKOR

'Angkor' is shorthand for the astonishing Hindu city and temple complex that was built in the jungle between the 10th and 12th centuries, when it was at the heart of a grand Khmer empire. Think Solomon, then add some. So immense were the building works they led to deforestation and flooding. A Chinese visitor in 1295 spoke of a golden tower and bridge, long verandas, mirror-filled halls. Contemporary inscriptions describe a festival in which 165,000 wax candles were used at one time. Floors were made of silver; each of hundreds of concubines wore a ruby necklace. Angkor is one of the wonders of the world.

After a colourful history, Angkor was sacked by the Thai in the 14th century in an epic jungle battle involving war-elephants, machines that fired multiple arrows, and rockets. Khmer wealth and building skills shifted to Ayutthaya in Thailand, as we have seen. What was left of Cambodia's ruling class moved south to the recently founded city of Phnom Penh. Buddhism appears to have finally taken over from Hinduism as the predominant faith around that time and Cambodia became something of a rural backwater. The French made it a protectorate in 1864.

ANGKAR

Angkar was 'The Organisation', the sinister name for the Khmer Rouge or Cambodian Communist Party, headed by Pol Pot, 'elder brother number one'. For a few terrible years in the 1970s *Angkar* put Cambodia in the same grisly league for killing its own people as Stalin's Russia and Mao's China.

In the far-off Angkor days, the Khmer people were the great empire, ruling over the Thai and the precursors to the Vietnamese. In the more recent *Angkar* days, it was almost as if all the evils and cruelties of the cold war came to roost on Cambodia's flat plains: bombed by the Americans, decimated by the Chinese-backed Khmer Rouge, 'liberated' by the Russian-backed Vietnamese. Cambodia's then head of state, Prince Sihanouk, saw those terrible times as the fulfilment of a fatalistic proverb familiar in the whole region: *flee from the tiger — the crocodile will eat you.*

You can outline the *Angkar* story in a few numbers and dates:

539,129: The number of tons of bombs dropped by American aeroplanes on Cambodia between 1969 and 1973. The North Vietnamese were using Cambodia as a supply route, and the illegal bombings were a doomed attempt to stop America losing the Vietnam War. By 1973, the Communist cause in Cambodia was greatly strengthened, and the Americans had killed tens of thousands of Cambodians.[23]

April 17 1975: The day Cambodia's capital Phnom Penh was 'liberated' by the Khmer Rouge, a communist outfit who believed that Cambodia's salvation lay in collectivised agriculture. Cities, hospitals, schools, libraries, and money were all scrapped, and everyone was sent off to construct a rural idyll, under the watchful guns of the liberators.

Three years, eight months, 20 days: The length of time the Khmer Rouge were in power. Each of those days, on average, they caused well over a thousand people to die. First killed were those in authority, then army officers, the educated, those wearing glasses, monks, Christians. True to the rural vision, most were battered with hoes. Many others fell sick and died though hard labour, disease and malnutrition. As grand irrigation schemes collapsed and the rural idyll failed to materialise, *Angkar* began to kill its own people.

Christmas Day 1978: The day the Vietnamese invasion began, which quickly destroyed *Angkar.* On the principle that 'my enemy's enemy is my friend', some Western countries and China continued to support the Khmer Rouge as it fought a guerrilla war against the Vietnamese. In this period the Khmer Rouge buried

thousands of landmines in Cambodia's most fertile fields, smuggled gems and illegally chopped down trees to sell to Thai loggers. Hundreds of thousands of Cambodians became refugees or, still worse, were driven through the jungles by the Khmer Rouge like cattle.

1.7 million: A commonly accepted estimate for the number of Cambodians whom *Angkar* killed, 20% of the Cambodian population. It may be more.

FISH EAT ANTS, ANTS EAT FISH

Aside from these dramatic appearances on the world stage, the Khmer followed the same rhythms for centuries, fishing and growing rice. The Mekong is Cambodia's great river. In the wet season, the Mekong overflows into a massive lake at the heart of Cambodia, the Tonle Sap. In the dry season, the Tonle Sap empties itself back into the Mekong. Hence the Khmer proverb: *Waters rise, fish eat ants; waters fall, ants eat fish,* the seasons go back and forth, nothing changes, death reigns. The fishing and farming techniques that are pictured in Angkor carvings were maintained undisrupted until the *Angkar* mayhem; supposedly an endless cycle.

Angkar ended all that. Today, though Cambodia remains poor, corrupt, and has a fragile democracy, it also has a future.

Let's look at:

• Cambodia today

• The Church

CAMBODIA TODAY

Standard measures of wealth and poverty put Cambodia alongside Myanmar and Laos as about the poorest countries of East Asia (only Timor-Leste is worse) and among the poorer countries of the world. In 2004 it was ranked 130th out of 177 in the Human Development Index, a broad measure of quality-of-life indicators. Cambodia is climbing up the Index. How long this continues depends on who wins the contest between corruption and nation-building.

The list of problems facing the Cambodian people is long, sad and mostly linked to poverty in its various forms: Too few well-educated leaders — a consequence of the earlier genocide ... half-completed buildings and roads, the funding all spent ... teachers and doctors paid much less than factory workers ... the forests chopped down illegally and the lakes and rivers overfished ... struggles to see democracy established ... economic growth resting precariously on foreign aid, tourism, and the garment industry.

Poverty begets poverty: unbuilt roads mean farmers can't get crops to market, underpaid teachers mean children can't get an education, unsatisfactory health services mean that sickness or disability leads to debt or death.

Perhaps because of its brutal recent past, Cambodia is also a violent place. Small quarrels are sometimes settled with machine guns. Domestic violence is common: a survey found 16% of women had suffered domestic violence from their spouses; half of these resulted in injuries, frequently to the head. Domestic sexual abuse of children, often highest among disempowered people wherever they are found in the world, is high in Cambodia, which in turn leads to a supply of sexually broken kids ripe for exploitation by the tourist trade.[24]

THE BATTLE FOR THE HEART

The real struggle for Cambodia's future, however, is not economic but in the hearts and minds of Cambodians. Princess Norodom Vacheahra is a member of the royal family who will at times criticize Cambodian politicians. She has

said, 'In just a few years, if well-managed and led by decent men who respect transparency and the rule of law, Cambodia would no longer ask donors for millions of dollars.'[25] The government needs our prayers.

Some of the Non-Governmental Organizations (NGOs) at work in Cambodia also see the battle for Cambodia's recovery in terms of heart-attitude. A recent Oxfam survey claimed that 'rebuilding trust at all levels of society is the overarching theme'.[26] An expatriate working in education laments that his students instinctively think they must cheat the system if they are to pass their exams.

As well as lack of trust, we might point out:

• Traditional fatalism and resignation — the true essence of poverty. This was underlined by the political terror of *Angkar* days. Meas Nee, a Cambodian community development worker (who is also a Christian) explained: 'My memories of that time are of feeling numb, just trying to stay alive, never to think. Not even to think when people were taken from the road and killed right where I was. I couldn't help so I didn't think.'[27]

- Fear — still ingrained among those who survived the Killing Fields; but also fear of evil spirits.

- Anger — because justice has not been done in Cambodia, and perhaps also because the traditional solutions, that involve suppressing or ignoring the problem, don't satisfy the soul.

- Loss of personal dignity, self-esteem, and self-confidence.

BEWARE AID

If all this is correct, a well-meaning world needs to beware of how it tries to serve Cambodia with foreign aid. Everything that encourages Cambodians to be grateful receivers of foreign munificence may reinforce a sense of powerlessness and poor self-esteem, the very thing that is at the heart of the nation's problems.

One of the more hopeful signs in Cambodia is the way hundreds of villages have set up 'Village Development Committees'. The aim of a VDC is to give the poor in a single place a united voice. It is quite a step of faith to trust one's neighbours after the betrayals of the Angkar era. But different VDCs have taken on loggers, set up rice-banks, run micro-credit schemes, taught literacy, and in doing so, tackled fear and disempowerment.

THE CHURCH

The Church's story weaves intriguingly through this larger story. For many years the Khmer showed much the same response to the gospel as did the Thai and the Burman. Protestant missions started late (1923) and the resulting Church was small, slow-growing and frequently persecuted.

Cambodia's troubles around the Angkar era changed all that. As described in Don Cormack's classic book Killing Fields, Living Fields, the Cambodian Church burst into extraordinary bloom, not once, but twice.

Phnom Penh saw a revival in the final months before the Khmer Rouge took over. In those few months the Church grew from several hundred to something like five thousand people — a widespread turning to Christ in repentance and faith just before Cambodia's holocaust. A year or two later, 70% of these new Christians would be dead.

A second Christian movement occurred in the refugee camps on the Thai borders at the end of the *Angkar* period. Since the refugee camps were transit camps, the churches that started in the camps were more like temporary revival meetings than true churches. Thousands responded, many fell away, but some didn't, and the many Cambodian churches that have grown up around the world are a lasting legacy.

In Cambodia itself, a number of Christians survived *Angkar* by various miraculous means. The Vietnamese invasion brought relief of a kind, but no freedom for Christian worship and the few Christians left were obliged to meet in secret through the 1980s.

Freedom finally came with the ending of the Cold War, the 1991 peace agreements, and the acceptance of the Christian faith as one of the official religions of the Cambodian state. 1991 was the beginning of a new day for Cambodia. And the Church began to grow rapidly soon afterwards.

EXPANSION

In such early days of a Christian movement, we should treat all statistics as provisional and slightly beside the point. But the church community (including children) may have grown from around 1000 in 1992 to 100,000 in 2002. A consultation between different church groups in 2002 counted 2,000 individual congregations. Whatever the true figures may be, something unusual and remarkable is happening, unique among the major Buddhist peoples on the banks of the Mekong. Cambodia, in so many ways one of 'the last' among these nations, may be one of 'the first' in terms of its response to Jesus.

All the limbs of a fully formed Christian movement are now growing and forming: Bible schools, theological education by extension for rural areas, youth work, Bible translation, networking meetings between different

groups, days of prayer. Christians who were victims of the Khmer Rouge have started churches in Khmer Rouge strongholds, reaching out to their former enemies in forgiveness.

The Cambodian Church is also notable for its holism, seeing its service to the community both in terms of sharing the gospel and caring for the vulnerable.[28]

But the Cambodian Church, more than anything, is *young*. Individual Christians who have walked with the Lord since, say, the 1960s or 1970s are very rare. Long-established Cambodian Christian traditions are non-existent. This is a Church without a past. A Church so suddenly born in this region is a cause for Christians to celebrate. But the young Church is vulnerable, doubly so because it is born among a vulnerable people, and not the least of the difficulties it faces is at the hands of its friends.

MANY NGOS ...

Along with the church growth has come a swarm of NGOs. Cambodia may indeed be the most 'NGO-ed' country in the world. In Cambodia you will find Christians involved in helping to rebuild the country's infrastucture, education, health and economy. It may be that something like a quarter of all the NGO work in Cambodia is Christian-inspired.

We can praise God for this. At heart it is a generous expression of Christian community and service. The intention is the fully rounded application of the Kingdom of God that Jesus himself embodied: heal the sick, open the eyes of the blind, free the oppressed, bring and be good news to the poor. And in Cambodia you will find many examples of outstanding Christian servants and institutions. Here's a grab bag of some of the excellent work going on — by no means comprehensive.[29]

1. Servants to Asia's Urban Poor have localized the management of their work with HIV/AIDS to a local organization called TASK. They provide an excellent community-based programme caring for 700 orphans.

2. Resource Development International and Tearfund have got together a consortium of NGOs working on HIV/AIDS and child abuse to produce Karaoke video training packs containing a series of workshops for children and youth.

3. Business for Mission is a consortium of Christian NGO business ventures seeking to foster socially responsible businesses such as Hagar (soya milk factory), Rajana (paper and garment design), Metalworks (metalwork design) and Yejj (computer/IT and café business). As well as providing work for vulnerable youth they also provide a model of non-corruption in a situation where corruption is the norm.

4. Chab Dai (Hands Together) is a network of 15 Christian organizations seeking to address the issue of sexual abuse and exploitation through advocacy, prevention, rescue and after-care.

5. Christian Peacebuilding Services is modelling ways of resolving conflicts other than by violence.

Christians are also doing about a quarter of the total work among Phnom Penh's street children. A Christian group has started pioneering work among released prisoners — no-one else is doing this. Some Christian NGOs like Harvest International Services are doing fine work in community health education. Lepers are being helped to care for themselves, again by Christians and a further demonstration of the old truth that 'atheists don't run leper colonies'. One innovative Christian group flies in a group of orthodontists from Scotland to train Cambodian dentists. The long list goes on.

... AND MANY PROBLEMS

But it isn't easy. The Christian groups vary in quality (so, of course do the non-Christian NGOs). And where Christian NGOs have weaknesses, Cambodian conditions will magnify them. Here are some reasons why:

1. *Patronage.* Deep in Khmer culture is the idea that if you're poor, you don't need a job, you need a patron. The patron looks after you and you, in exchange, do his bidding. Cambodia can be the land of the instant ministry. Arrive with sufficient funds and you can easily buy up a large house, some Christian Khmer staff, and plenty of photogenically needy children. You can set up and lead your own Bible college. Would-be apostles can even set up an instant denomination: it is said there are church congregations who will change affiliation and even rewrite their statements of faith if some new source of patronage looks juicy enough.

2. *Divisiveness.* A second consequence of the perceived struggle for foreign funds and patronage is the jostling to be counted as Cambodia's most strategic, best, leading, central Christian group. At the last count, Cambodia's relatively small Christian community had six wannabe umbrella Church councils, each seeking to be the foremost representative of Khmer Christianity. One of the smaller ones has been accused of trying to bribe the government to gain recognition. Further divides occur between Cambodian Christians who grew up overseas and those who never left.

So, in the midst of a turning to Christ that is a rare and precious event in a Buddhist nation, and in the midst of large and generous giving from the Church worldwide, there is plenty of background noise as unspiritual egos and superspiritual ambitions crunch against each other and large amounts of money are doled out.

It isn't hard to find echoes here of certain New Testament situations. One can imagine Paul writing to some Cambodian groups as he wrote to the young Corinthian church:

You gladly put up with fools because you are so wise! In fact, you even put up with anyone who enslaves you or exploits you or takes advantage of you or pushes himself forward or slaps you in the face. To my shame I admit that we were too weak for that.[32]

Beware, then, sectarian, foreign-agenda-driven Christian groups who are more interested in photos for their magazines than seeing the Cambodian Christian community standing on its own feet, free, secure, matured and confident in Christ. The small, the partial and the patient are often better models for effective NGO ministry than the grandiose.

LAST WORD

There's another old saying about fish: *give a person a fish and you feed them for a day. Teach a person to fish and you will feed them for a lifetime.* This, however, is sub-Christian. Let the gospel take hold of someone, and they might start thinking a little bit beyond their family's food supplies. They might start living outward-looking lives of service, rather than inward-looking lives of survival. The Christian gospel, embodied in Christian lives, is surely the deep remedy that can genuinely transform Cambodia. But this is only the start.

The burgeoning Christian movement in Cambodia is so exciting, so much the thing that prior generations of Christians have longed to see. Yet now more than ever it needs all the unfashionable attributes of apostleship applied to it to make it strong: patience, faith, humility, voluntary vulnerability and powerlessness. Paul wrote to a church in Corinth that was dazzled by flashy apostles: 'Death works in us, life in you.' Thank God for those locals and foreigners who are treading out that path: pray for many more of them.

LAOS

Laos is poor, small, and mountainous. As often with mountainous countries, it is home to many small peoples: 138 by one count. The majority are Thai-related, a third are Khmer-related and another sizeable minority are related to the Hmong, one of the minorities in Vietnam who have seen the greatest response to the gospel.

A permanent Protestant missionary presence only came to Laos in 1902. The Church is small with an evangelical community of around 40,000 in a population of around 6m. It is concentrated among tribal groups like the Khmu, Hmong, Bru and Ta Oy. Most other groups remain out of reach of the gospel. No missionaries are allowed.

Lao's Communist government dances to a Vietnamese tune and is a repressive, somewhat paranoid one-party state. There is a sporadic and unsuccessful resistance movement trying to overthrow the government, and, overseas, a rather better organized movement among the Hmong people.

Most of the Christians belong to peoples like the Hmong who are associated with the anti-government movements. The Hmong, indeed, were famous in the Vietnam war as being the CIA's private army. Observers are at pains to stress that local Christians are not involved in the anti-government movements. For some years, however, the state has treated the Christian faith as a political threat, and savagely persecuted the Church.

In recent years the persecution has taken the form of government officials visiting a village and asking believers to sign a form which says:

'I _____ do formally request to resign from Jesus' religion and will stop:
1. Praying, singing, reading the Bible
2. Praying for the sick
3. Praying before meals
4. Changing names.
If I violate this undertaking, I request higher levels to punish me.

Between 1998 and 2003 as many as 80% of the tribal believers in some provinces were presented with forms to sign. Those who refused were threatened, jailed, beaten and deprived of their land. Families suffered just as much as the head of the household.[30] Laos was named as number three in the world's worse persecutors of Christians in January 2004, topped only for cruelty and brutality by North Korea and Saudi Arabia.[31]

Some indications are that this persecution was easing in 2004. Meanwhile, Chinese housechurches are making plans to bring the gospel to unreached groups in Northern Laos. And the Church is reported to be growing in the capital, Vientiane, and in some of the provinces.

VIETNAM

Space forbids us to say much about Vietnam, which is politically and culturally much closer to China than the other South East Asian countries: the north of Vietnam was a province of China for about 1000 years. It has been rather neglected by Protestant missions, with permanent work starting only in 1911, through the Christian & Missionary Alliance.

Vietnam is huge — about the size of Italy and with the population of Germany. It is poor, but the economy is growing almost as fast as China's and with a similar dramatic effect on the (growing and young) population. In 1993 the World Bank concluded that nearly 60% of its people were poor. In 2002, thanks to foreign investment and land reform, that figure was 29%. The cities are booming, China-style, at the expense of the country.

It has been a Communist state since the North Vietnamese defeated the American-backed South in 1975. Expatriate Protestant missionaries, of whom there were never more than about 300, were expelled that same year. A number were martyred in the years up to 1975.

As in China, the Vietnamese Communists face the tension of maintaining themselves in power while simultaneously opening their economy to the free market.

All religions are frowned upon. The Vietnamese seek to control Christianity by regulating a few official churches, and stamping down hard on the rest. Open evangelism is forbidden. There are perhaps 300 official Protestant congregations and several thousand illegal, underground ones.[32] Both the official and unofficial churches are growing. The Catholic Church is about four times bigger than the Protestant, and also suffers severe restrictions, particularly in recruiting and training new clergy.

Most of the churches are made up of tribal people from Vietnam's Central Highlands. In Vietnam these people are still known by the French term 'Montagnard'. As everywhere in South East Asia, the tribal peoples are poor, marginalized, and more likely to turn to Christ. So the persecution of Montagnard Christians is actually racial and religious discrimination shaded together. Some of the 'persecutions' are better understood as crackdowns on political protest among the Montagnards.

But the Christian tribal peoples are

clearly suffering for their faith. One well-placed informant wrote:

The campaign to stop and reverse the movement to Christian faith among Vietnam's minority people is growing. There appears to be a strong widespread effort that uses the same ideology, from Vietnam's far northern provinces down to the central highlands. The ideology used is the relatively new policy of promoting the traditional culture and values. In the name of this policy, Christian tribal people are hounded sometimes literally to death, because they will not return to animistic practices such as ancestor worship, animal sacrifices, drinking blood, drunkenness and immorality.

Those who refuse to renounce their faith have been internally exiled, beaten or jailed. Some have died from their beatings. People from mostly Christian villages have also had to flee into the jungle when large numbers of Vietnamese security people arrived to burn and loot.

The harshness of the Vietnamese state's treatment of its Christians has only apparently increased the stubbornness of the Christians. The Protestant Church, which is perhaps 1.2m strong when calculated at its widest (about 1.5% of the population) is growing fast.

Among the many needs are:

- Freedom from persecution, a freedom that might enable the Church to train leaders and tackle internal division and heresy. The country's only official theological training college opened in 2003. Bibles, children's material, study aids, and scripture translations into minority languages are all severely lacking.

- Pioneering work in North Vietnam, which has seen less exposure to the gospel — though as many as 150,000 Hmong tribespeople have become Christians through Christian radio broadcasts.

- Evangelism for the new generation — a people very eager to leave behind Vietnam's old ways, to work hard, study, get rich, and adopt the lifestyles of the wealthier people of Asia and the West. Their openness to new ideas is striking, and may not last forever.

Vietnam craves international respectability and does not like — for example — people standing outside its embassies around the world with lists of Christian prisoners and grievances. On his release, one imprisoned pastor reported that he had received over 4000 letters in prison, from 55 countries.[33]

- 4 -

Japan

Japanese culture is what stands between Japanese people and the gospel. The same cultural elements that hold the nation together and make it strong have so far kept the gospel out. Let's tentatively try to sketch some of these, by leafing through Japan's past.

INGREDIENTS FOR A NATION

Shinto. Japan's indigenous faith stretches back beyond recorded history. Shinto means 'the way of *kami*' where *kami* means something like 'superior' or 'divinity' or 'divine power'. All kinds of things possess *kami*: mountains and rivers, great people, and abstract concepts such as growth or creation. Shinto is the set of rituals and traditions that are felt to ease the Japanese through a *kami*-filled life.

Like superstitions in the West, these stone-age Japanese beliefs have persisted into a post-modern era. When the bullet trains pass Mount Fuji, they slow down and the guards bow to the great mountain. Newborns are welcomed with Shinto rites; stages in a child's growth are marked off with them. Taking part in Shinto offerings is part of the job-description of many a Japanese middle-manager — you can't launch a ship, or a product, or a new year, without the right rite. *Kami* is what the Emperor was forced to admit to not having, as the price of staying on his throne after the Japanese defeat in 1945. Most Japanese claim not actually to believe in a God or gods and keep Shinto at arm's length; but the Shinto patterns and habits die hard.

Borrowing from the Chinese. Early Japan was shaped by Chinese influence, especially during China's mighty T'ang dynasty (618-907). Buddhism came over and filled in the gaps that Shinto left. Today, Buddhism does family, funerals and ancestors; Shinto does nation, birth and youth. Ideas of

harmony, balance and simplicity, mediated to Japan through Buddhism, created wonderful art, architecture, landscaping and literature. Buddhism's eightfold path brought a moral component that Shinto lacked. And Buddhist philosophy forever coloured Japanese thought with ideas of the transience of people in a meaningless universe. The thought of emptiness or non-existence as the final human state is much more attractive to many Japanese than the rather terrifying notion of 'eternal life'.

The honour code. Japanese borrowing from China declined as the Chinese T'ang dynasty weakened and fell. Japan's Heian period (794-1185) was Japan's own golden era. By the end of that period, real power had shifted from the Emperor to various noble families and Buddhist sects, each with private armies.

This feudal period in Japan lasted from the mid-12th to the mid-19th centuries. In between civil wars, it led to people being appointed *shogun* by the Emperor. (The word is an abbreviated form of *seii tai-shogun* or 'barbarian-suppressing supreme general.'[35]) The shoguns held the real power. Underneath them were the knightly class of *samurai* warriors.

The *samurai*, much like their equivalents in early mediaeval Europe, were seen as defining the honour code for the nation. In Japan this included ideas like loyalty to one's feudal lord as being more important than loyalty to family; personal honour being more important than life itself; and ritual suicide being an honourable exit from shame. Death preferable to shame; the group more important than the individual: there are still echoes of the *samurai* honour code in Japan today.

Appearance is everything. In the seventeenth century, Ieyasu Tokugawa, founder of the Tokugawa shogunate (1603-1868) took severe

> 'To be a Japanese is to live always in dread of what others think of you.'[47]

measures to retain a grip on a country that was being destabilised by foreign influences — including Christianity, as we shall see.

The Tokugawa shogunate sealed Japan off from the rest of the world for 250 years and created what would be called today a police state. Travel, clothing, houses, diet were all regulated. Bridges were destroyed to weaken internal communications. Whole families died for the guilt of an individual.

Two-and-a-half centuries of this kind of rule leave a mark. The sense of Christianity being foreign and unJapanese is one such mark. A deeper one — according to some observers — is the ingrained cultural habit of *honne* and *tatamae*, literally *'inner reality'* and *'outward appearance'*. Under the Tokugawa shogunate, outward appearance was all. Communities and families had to appear harmonious, loyal and peaceable: lives depended on it. Even today, how something appears on the outside is more important in Japan than what privately it truly is. The culture that has developed the most beautiful gift-wrapping on earth gift-wraps itself.

Borrowing from the West. In 1853 Commodore Matthew Perry of the United States Navy sailed into Japan to open the country for trade and diplomacy. Japan was powerless to stop this foreign intervention, and that was a great shock for a proud nation.

Yet Japan responded with great vigour. The last Tokugawa *shogun* stood down to prevent anarchy, and the Emperor's direct rule was restored. The new boy-emperor named his reign the 'Meiji' ('Enlightened Rule') era. It featured wholesale Western-style reform involving land-ownership, education, banking, railways, electricity, even clothing and architectural styles. Japan became the first 'Asian tiger'. *Samurai* became unemployed, then redeployed as bureaucrats or businessmen.

National pride held the nation together through this shake-up — a remarkable testimony to the strength and vigour of Japanese culture. Many nations have crumbled under similar pressures.

Yet national pride went on to betray the nation. As the twentieth century unfolded, Japanese politics turned sharply rightward. The Emperor's position became ever more emphasized, as upholder of national stability and apex of Shinto devotion. What some writers have called *Japanism* — a devotion to the divine status of the Emperor and the nation that can be considered a kind of 'Shinto fundamentalism' — took hold. In 1937, for example, the Ministry of Education published a book called *Kokuta-no-Hongi* (*Cardinal Principles of the Nation*) which stressed self-sacrifice for the good of the nation and faith in the Emperor's divinity. Seek first the Japanese Empire, as it were, and everything will be added to you.

That sad principle, acting in a world that was itself inclined to nationalistic solutions, led to a trail of blood and rubble — via Nanking, Pearl Harbor, Okinawa — all the way to Hiroshima and Nagasaki.

Overtaking the West. At the end of the Second World War, Japan was occupied by foreign invaders for the first time in its history, and its cities had been bombed and burned by the fiercest weaponry ever deployed on human beings.

Yet Japan quickly regained its independence, rebuilt, and went on to create one of the most amazingly successful economies of all time. Dismiss for the moment recent stories of relative Japanese economic or moral decline. As well as being prosperous and leading the world in technology and infrastructure, Japan is a land of clean and safe and disabled-friendly streets, polite and hardworking people, low crime, little problem with drugs and few

children growing up without a family. Japanese people live longer than almost everyone else. Their country is beautiful. How can you not feel affection for a nation that broadcasts forecasts of the cherry-blossom opening so that no-one misses the onset of spring? Few countries are more generous with international aid. It has championed pacifism and never again sent its army into combat overseas.[36] And the trains run on time.

All this was built out of radioactive rubble within a single generation, testimony again to the extraordinary resilience of the Japanese nation.

STILL A STUMBLING BLOCK?

And yet many people wonder if pride in Japan's national strength and resourcefulness isn't again proving a stumbling block. It isn't too far-fetched to see Japan's post-war recovery as a struggle for the honour of the Japanese nation conducted now by businessmen instead of by soldiers. The *samurai* ethic of self-disciplined striving for victory runs deep — so does the fear of failure — and enforces long hours on workers, and fantastic pressures on students.

Japan has remained somewhat isolationist. It doesn't welcome immigrants or asylum seekers. And Japan has arguably not come to terms with its war guilt, beyond expressing a general regret that it all somehow happened. No-one inside Japan seems to know whose fault the war was. The museums at Hiroshima and Nagasaki treat the atomic bombs as if they fell randomly out of a blue sky.[37] Leading politicians still honour war criminals. And when a reporter once bravely asked the late wartime Showa Emperor if he took responsibility for the war, his reply was memorable: 'Since I am not an expert in literature I do not understand the nuance of the word responsibility.'[38]

All this may help to suggest reasons why the Christian faith might struggle for a foothold here. What does Japan need with a foreign faith, especially one that seems to come from countries awash with far more social problems than Japan has? How can a message like the gospel, that divides people, ever thrive when working together in harmony is so highly prized and has served the nation so well? Where does a call to repentance and humility fit when 'sin' is a strange concept and the cultural pressure is to hide everything shameful and show only unity and success?

CHURCH

So it has proved — almost. Christianity has only rarely thrived in Japan. But it has had its moments.

The story of Japan's encounter with Christianity starts a long way back. The Assyrian Church of the East claims that missionaries came to Japan within the first few centuries AD. That perhaps is yet to be proven. But there's good evidence that Christians from T'ang China did visit and made an impression.[39]

Then, in 1549, Francis Xavier and two other Jesuits landed at the southern tip of Japan, far-flung representatives of the Catholic missionary awakening. What followed has been called Japan's 'Christian century.' They and their successors baptized 150,000 people in the next forty years. Xavier is perhaps the only missionary in history to give himself baptism-related Repetitive Strain Injury.[40] Some of those baptized were prominent leaders. Possibly no other Asian civilisation responded so quickly and in such numbers to the Catholic missions. 'It seems to me,' said Xavier, 'that we shall never find ... a race to equal the Japanese.'

> Japan has a sense of being a nation divinely set apart. In the national Shinto myth, the current Emperor is number 125 in a direct line of descendants from the goddess Amaterasu. According to a book I have from the Japan Tourist Board, this version of the national story is 'still being debated by historians'.

There are human reasons for Catholicism's early success. The foreign missionaries were linked with Portuguese traders, who could supply exotic weapons. The ruling Shogun Nobunaga Oda (1543-1582) welcomed Christianity as a foil to the unruly Buddhist powers around him. When a feudal lord adopted Catholicism, it was natural for all his serfs to do so as well, boosting the numbers of baptisms.[41] And maybe Catholicism, with candles, incense, rosaries and flowers wasn't clearly separated in many minds from a version of Buddhism.

Yet the young Church that emerged showed a courage in martyrdom the equal of any group of Christians on earth. When the political tide turned and persecution fell, many stayed loyal to the faith, despite crucifixions, threats, and severe, state-run persecution. Even after 225 years, some distant form of Christianity was still being secretly held onto in the countryside around Nagasaki, as the Catholics discovered. They built a cathedral in Nagasaki in the nineteenth century and had four thousand Japanese from the nearby village of Urakami knocking at its doors. These people had waited a quarter of a millennium for the Church to return.[42]

There were similar ripples of interest in Christianity in later times of national weakness and uncertainty. The first Protestant missionaries arrived in 1859. In 1872 the Meiji government lifted its ban on Christianity and in the following unstable decade Christianity again became 'so popular that one prominent magistrate was prompted to predict that it might even be named the official state religion.'[43] But again, growing national confidence called people back to their roots and stemmed the flow of new Christians.

The same happened after the Second World War. In the turmoil and confusion of the early years, a number of Japanese people again reached toward Christianity. The Church had a numerical peak, at about 1.4% of the population in 1954. Since then, the growth curve has been flat and in 2003 the number of churches actually declined.

THE CHURCH TODAY

Today the Church stands out as an oddity within Japan, and suffers for it: Japan is not a land of oddities. Cultural pressure keeps people away from the churches, drives people out of them, and distorts what's left.

A Japanese Christian has to stand out from the group, whether it's in happy national Shinto festivals, family occasions, births or funerals; at work or school; on an almost daily basis. Christianity is unJapanese and it enforces unJapanese behaviour.

One Japanese woman who turned to Christ while studying in the USA described what it was like returning home:

After I returned to Japan, I attended church and other Christian activities regularly. [My parents'] concern was not about my faith, but was about my well-being in society … If I am too stubborn about my faith and don't conform to the society because of my religion, they were afraid that their daughter would be an outcast.[44]

This constant pressure takes its toll: as many as 80% of people who return home to Japan as Christians are said to fall away. The same kind of figure holds for people who turn to Christ in Japan.

'They start to become "quiet" Christians,' one missionary told me. 'Then they stop coming.' Even ones who appear stalwart Christians, of a number of years' standing, can turn back when their stage in life starts to demand Shinto or Buddhist responsibilities. 'I've enjoyed my years of freedom,' is a comment you hear sometimes. 'But now I've got to go back.'

The Japanese Church is also largely made up of women. The traditional Japanese urban way of life can be partly blamed here, with a corporate-warrior husband away from home for long hours and a wife underemployed and lonely at home. It can also be perceived that the Church is about developing what might be seen as traditional feminine qualities, like peacemaking, submission and forbearance, and this isn't necessarily attractive to the Japanese male. Church, it seems, is not for the brave or the strong.

Then, family commitments mean that the women in the church have split loyalties on the only day the whole family is together. Fewer than half of the members of a typical church actually attend on a given Sunday. But weekdays are no better for Christian meetings. The long hours and fast pace of urban Japanese life squeeze out the slow time that is needed to build Christian communities.

A Church so isolated within the prevailing culture can be pushed out of its normal shape, which can lead to further problems. Here are some issues which I'm told are common:

1. *Static:* In 2004, the Christian Databook counted the membership of Japan's 7,000 or so evangelical churches as '387,001'. The '1' is the scariest digit in that statistic, pointing to a church that is all-too-rigidly delineated. In Brazil, a country of a roughly similar population, the Assemblies of God once miscounted their flock by ten million souls. In the happy, rampant chaos that is China, no-one knows the size of the Church to the nearest 25 million. The Christian movement has yet to overwhelm those who count sheep in Japan.

2. *The* sensei *syndrome*. *Sensei* is the word Japanese use for *teacher*, and the 'syndrome' refers to the problem of church members becoming overly dependent on the pastor, rather than on the Lord Jesus. This can reflect a feature of Japanese groups which (Japanese authors will tell you) are organized around relationships rather than 'a rule'.[45] So your relationship to

Spoken Japanese is unrelated to spoken Chinese, so using Chinese characters to write Japanese words posed problems that were only solved by inventing phonetic alphabets (*katakana* and *hiragana*) for awkward words. Japan's likeable habit of incorporating into its language the unincorporable from elsewhere continues today with such enjoyable creations as *sarariman* (corporate salary-man or 'suit'), *boi-furendo* (boyfriend) or *makudonarudo* (the twin golden arches).

the pastor is more important than your own walk with God. It doesn't help that ministers who have worked and prayed long to see a single member added to the church can in turn be accused of being somewhat overprotective of their new lamb. The *sensei* syndrome can stunt normal Christian growth. People let the pastor do their thinking for them, and that sharply restricts the creativity and responsiveness of the whole Church. It can also hamper inter-church relations, for the fear of pastors losing their flock to another church. Over-dependence on leaders is also how cults get started. At the same time, there is a shortage of church leaders, and a generation of them is passing away. At the time of writing, over 75% of Japanese pastors were aged 55 or more. Fresh models of leadership are urgently needed.

3. The self-sustaining problems of isolated churches. Isolation can lead to a kind of discontinuity with the outside world, which in turn can lead to legalism and further isolation. Add to that the fact that Japanese are taught from their mother's knee to conform and it becomes very hard for Christians to take the risk of engaging with the surrounding culture. So for example, many of the radical experiments in youth work, worship or church planting that are a somewhat familiar part of the scene even in the not-very-healthy Western Church are extremely rare in Japan.

PROSPECTS

In a sense, then, the great strengths of the Japanese nation and people seem to be directed against the gospel getting a hearing or winning hearts in that nation. But that is, of course, the same as everywhere in the world. Every human culture opposes the gospel. Yet every human culture will yield its treasures to the gospel. The problem is always with the timing. Workers in Japan are at the moment called to be faithful in unresponsive times. Here are some of the things that can encourage them.

1. *Life is life.* For all that we have said about cultural pressures against the gospel, genuine spiritual life still makes its mark in Japan. Locals and foreigners alike actually can see people turn to Christ, have their lives changed, and serve him all their lives in a church that, as a community, reflects something of Jesus to those who encounter it. The gospel is still the greatest power on earth and it still works.

2. *The welcome.* Japan has freedom of religion and its people are often interested in discussing the Christian faith. Japan welcomes Christian workers on missionary visas. And it's a lovely place to live, once, as a foreigner, you've accustomed yourself to a lifetime of language and culture learning.

3. *The slow thaw.* Japanese churches are, slowly, finding ways to work together, and are seeing a parallel improvement in their health. Mission agencies are recognizing the value of church-planting teams, rather than sending a single person or couple. There are local, regional and national get-togethers, for example on the theme of starting churches, which signifies an improvement on previous decades. Popular evangelists or speakers can attract interdenominational crowds in their thousands. Welcome though all this is, it has to be understood as only a slow thaw from a deep freeze.

4. *New streams.* The current standard model of church life in Japan — a pastor, a building, a small Sunday congregation mostly of women and children — urgently needs either an upgrade or at least some additional streams of Christian life alongside it. There are some creative ideas.

The 'VIP' ministry is perhaps the most striking. This is an outreach to businessmen, somewhat on the lines of the 'Full Gospel Businessmen's Fellowship' in that it invites prestigious Christian speakers to address ticket-buying audiences of men around a restaurant meal. Workplace Bible studies follow. It has become a lifeline for Christian corporate warriors and some high-profile people are associated with it — the current Governor of the Bank of Japan, for example. There's now a chapter reaching Japanese businessmen in the City of London. As a fresh stream of Christian influence reaching into the heart of Japanese life, VIP is a remarkable development.

I heard of other interesting ideas. A Christian pastor bought some land for a cemetery and told the local community that the church would tend the graves of any that chose to be buried there. This proved surprisingly attractive to a generation that today worries about who will tend its graves. He then started a 'silver' (ie grey-haired) Bible study among his prospective cemetery customers. Not many Christian ministries have started with dead people and worked backwards — most start with children and work forwards — but it could catch on in a country that will have a quarter of its population aged over 65 within a few years.

The internet offers a way for people to explore the Christian faith without having to publicly identify with a church, and a small number of people are finding Christian friendship in chat rooms. I have heard reports of people coming to faith as a result.

One missionary, Patrick McElligott of WEC, had practically a national ministry speaking about family life to Parent-Teacher Association meetings. Work like this strengthened the Christian movement in many ways: it encouraged many solitary Christians, led directly to a few conversions, and moved thousands of people forward in their appreciation of the gospel.

Other people are speculating with the idea of 'Basic church' or 'simple church'[46] which might be understood as a variant of the cell-church movement, only without the central large meeting. (Of course it is a set of ideas cropping up worldwide, not restricted to or originating from Japan.) Here the idea is to dispense with buildings, pastors, congregations and the whole traditional infrastructure and simply redefine 'church' as any small group of people meeting around the Bible, any day, any context. When the small group grows too big, divide it into two. (In the jargon, this kind of division is known as 'multiplication'.)

When you apply 'simple church' ideas to, say, the VIP movement, the VIP Bible studies suddenly become churches and you don't bother trying to force businessmen into unfamiliar pews on Sundays before they can become proper

Christians. 'Simple church' ideas may help free Japanese Christianity from its bondage to Western worship times, songs, buildings, and culture.

THE CHANGING JAPAN

A bigger trend is that Japan is slowly becoming less like Japan, and more like everywhere else. Work is less all-consuming than for a previous generation: higher unemployment, the growth of a leisure industry, the increase in the number of public holidays, a culture of somewhat shorter working hours, all point to more free time.

The number of Shinto temples is slowly decreasing, and for all the millions who will be found enjoying the winter sunshine at a beautiful shrine in the New Year, many will also be crowding into airports to get away.

The younger generation is widely thought to be disenchanted with the lives laid out for them by their culture, a cause of concern to many in Japan. Many truant from school, some refusing even to leave their rooms. The rise in the number of job agencies point to a change in working culture: jobs are neither offered nor taken for life, and people look for more from a career than long years in a suit.

Especially, young Japanese women appear to be unenamoured by the current expectation to study hard, marry well, and then spend many years treading carefully around a workaholic husband and his aged relatives. The divorce rate rose by half between 1990 and 1998 and fewer Japanese women of marriageable age are bothering to marry at all. One survey reported, 'Far nicer to go on living rent-free with her own parents as a "parasite single", or become a "freeter" — one who drifts from job to job rather than settling down to conventional employment. Some 10% of the 15m unmarried Japanese aged 20-34 are freeters.'

The ever-turning kaleidoscope of culture may indeed be starting to open a new window of opportunity for the Church in Japan — though one that few people at the moment are doing anything about.

Amidst all their wealth, health, privilege and education there is a singular lostness or emptiness visible in Japanese young people. Some have joined the wierdest neo-Shinto cults. Some worship UFOs. Some take lessons in Western-style dating techniques. Some join choirs that sing gospel songs, in English. (There's a half-hour gospel choir show on national TV.) Most drift though a pick-and-mix world, over-educated, over-entertained and apparently looking for something though they perhaps don't know what.

A third or more of young Japanese who marry nowadays choose a 'Christian' (ie Western-style) wedding service. Such a service usually follows a pattern that begins with singing 'What a friend we have in Jesus' and lasts around twenty minutes. 'Christian' wedding chapels abound in Japan, mostly (it seems to me) notable for theme-park kitsch rather than spiritual vitality. In 'Christian' weddings, foreign pastors are preferred, and it's more important that they look good than that they are theologically orthodox, which explains why many 'wedding pastors' are bartenders or English teachers or other Western drifters earning some money on the side.

The value of this as a direct opportunity for the gospel is hard to call. Some missionaries take Christian weddings, arguing they can make the most of the opportunity by offering, for example, pre-wedding preparation courses. Others are distinctly dubious. It doesn't seem to result in too many disciples of Jesus — but then, what does?

It's a huge trend, however, and may even extend into other areas of life. If weddings, why not 'Christian funerals', western-style sendoffs that have a bit more style than the traditional Buddhist affairs? Non-Christian Japanese sometimes note with approval the hope and joy expressed in a Christian funeral.

As a commentary on younger Japanese people, however, the 'Christian wedding' phenomenon is hard to beat. It's kitsch and superficial. It's expensive and fashion-conscious. It's a turning away from the past, and from Japanese tradition. It's vague about the future. Perhaps, more speculatively, somewhere there's a seeking for a transcendence or a joy that wealth and high technology can't deliver. Perhaps, even more speculatively, there's an unspoken groping towards some 'new covenant' — some new agreement about what marriage, home, life, are all *for*.

SPEED THE DAY

Surely the God who rules over culture will one day make Japan ripe for the gospel, not (as it is today) barren. Perhaps that day is nearer than anyone suspects: who would have thought Japan's neighbours Korea or China could have embraced the gospel so fast and so widely in such a short time? And surely the quiet faithfulness of Japanese Christianity today and the prayers of Christians around the world will help bring that day forward. Will the Church be ready when the ripe opportunity comes round again? Let's hope so.

FURTHER READING

WEBSITES — GENERAL

A site by and for Buddhists with lots to explore including histories of Buddhism in Southeast Asia and Japan.
www.Buddhanet.net

The site of the Christian mission agency OMF international is a fine research resource for up-to-date news and summaries of all the countries in this book.
www.omf.org
www.onebillionwait.org

People who track the persecuted church have a special interest in Laos, Vietnam and Myanmar, for example:
Christian Solidarity International
www.csi-int.ch
Open Doors
www.od.org
Release International
www.releaseinternational.org
Amnesty International
www.amnesty.org
Human Rights Watch
www.hrw.org

WEBSITES — COUNTRY-SPECIFIC

Prayer news for Myanmar, though focussed mostly on the Karen and the other Christian tribal peoples
www.prayforburma.org

News of the local Christian response to the Asian tsunami in Thailand.
www.welovethailand.in.th

The site of the Christian agency SAO-Cambodia, it also contains background information and news on that country.
www.sao-cambodia.org

Training and resources for Christians reaching Japanese with the gospel. US-based; a ministry of Campus Crusade for Christ.
www.thejapannet.com

Devoted to helping Japanese Christian returnees integrate back into Japan.
www.jcfn.org

NEWSPAPERS

Cambodia

Phnom Penh Post, twice monthly.
www.phnompenhpost.com
Cambodia Daily
www.camnet.com.kh/cambodia.daily

Laos

Vientiane Times

English language newspaper including, oddly, the phone numbers of leading politicians.
www.vientianetimes.com

Myanmar

New Light of Myanmar

Official newspaper, full of accounts of ministers visiting sugar cane factories.
www.myanmar.com

Democratic Voice of Burma

Independent reporting.
www.dvb.no

Burma Project

Plenty of background information to mobilize people to campaign for political change.

www.burmaproject.org

Thailand

Bangkok Post
www.bangkokpost.com

Thailand Daily

World News Network site, rich source of varied information.
www.thailanddaily.com

Japan

Asahi Daily

Linked to the International Herald Tribune.
www.asahi.com/english

The Daily Yomiuri

News site with culture and other links.
www.yomiuri.co.jp

Vietnam

Viet Nam news
vietnamnews.vnagency.com.vn

PRAYER GUIDES

A Prayer a Day for Myanmar

31-day prayer guide for Myanmar produced by a coalition of mission agencies and available to purchase or download. Various languages.
www.p4mm.com

30 Days of Prayer for Laos

Available to order from OMF, among others.
www.omf.org/p4laos

Free Japan

Website to promotion intercession for Japan, plenty of articles and a useful 31-day prayer plan. Attempts to co-ordinate united prayer for revival in Japan.
www.freejapan.org

BOOKS — GENERAL

Bowers, Dr Russell (ed.)

2003 *Folk Buddhism in Southeast Asia* (Cambodia: Training of Timothys). An introduction from a Christian perspective to aspects of folk Buddhism. It may be possible to obtain this book via World Vision, for whom it was originally produced.

Hattaway, Paul

2004 *Peoples of the Buddhist World: A Christian Prayer Guide* (UK: Piquant). The definitive prayer guide to Buddhist peoples; a major step forward for missions to the Buddhist world. Best obtained direct from www.asiaharvest.org

BOOKS — COUNTRY-SPECIFIC

Brown, Ian

2000 *Cambodia* (An Oxfam Country Profile) (Oxfam GB). Highlights development issues in Cambodia through the stories of several individuals.

Cormack, Don

1997 *Killing Fields Living Fields* (UK: MARC). The classic history of the Cambodian Church.

Endo, Shusako

Silence. Classic fiction written by a Japanese Catholic, based around the true story of two Jesuits who apostasized after being tortured.

Himm, SokReaksa S

2003 *The Tears of My Soul* (UK: Monarch/SAO Cambodia). Biography of a survivor from the Khmer Rouge era.

Japan Evangelical Missionary Association (JEMA)

2000 *Operation Japan* published by the Operation Japan Publishing Committee and JEMA. For copies of this handbook for prayer contact: Japanese Evangelical Missionary Society, 201 South, Sante Fe #307, Los Angeles, CA 90012, USA.

Lewis, David C

1993 *The Unseen Face of Japan* (UK: Monarch). A Christian anthropologist studies Shinto.

McElligott, Patrick

2002 *On Giants' Shoulders* (UK: Ambassador Publications). Memoirs of a church planter in Japan who saw considerable success in his ministry.

Mawdsley, James

2001 *The Heart Must Break (the fight for democracy and truth in Burma)* (UK: Random House). The story of a one-man human rights campaign in Myanmar.

Mullins, Mark R

1998 *Christianity Made in Japan* (University of Hawaii Press). A study of indigenous Japanese Christian movements.

Thwe, Pascal Khoo

2003 *From the Land of Green Ghosts* (UK: Harper Collins). Story of a Burmese tribal Catholic who takes a degree in English literature in Cambridge: unique, insightful, cross-cultural perspective.

Ponchaud, Francois

Cambodia: Year Zero and Cathedral of the Rice Paddies. Hard-to-obtain classics from a French Catholic priest who served in Cambodia.

NOTES

1 Pascal Khoo Thwe *From the Land of Green Ghosts* (London: Harper Collins 2002), p 63.

2 The links between Buddhism and the physics of the very small are many and intriguing.

3 John R. Davies *The Path to Enlightenment* (London: Hodder and Stoughton 1997), p 38.

4 OMF's magazine *East Asia's Billions*, Oct 2001, p 4.

CHAPTER 1 MYANMAR

5 Nick Danziger in *Time* 19-26 August, 2002.

6 Christian Solidarity Worldwide visit report, November 2002, p 13.

7 *Economist* Jan 24 2004, p 54.

8 I'm indebted to Don Richardson's classic book *Eternity in their Hearts* (1984, Gospel Light) for these examples.

9 See *A prayer a day for Myanmar*, an inter-agency prayer guide, available from www.p4mm.com.

10 *Operation World* figures, though there is little consensus among Christian groups as to how many Christians there actually are in Myanmar.

11 James Mawdsley, *The Heart Must Break (the fight for democracy and truth in Burma)*, (London: Random House 2001), p 197.

CHAPTER 2 THAILAND

12 According to a history of missions to the Thai published on www.ywamthai.org/office/religion.htm.

13 Nancy Ashcraft *Yours Crusading, WEC in Thailand 1952-1956*, unpublished manuscript in the possession of WEC International, p 89.

14 Brenda G Holton in the OMF newsletter *Praying for Thailand*, July 2003.

15 From 'Shedding the weight of spirit worship', Bible Society, October 2001. www.biblesociety.org/wr_363/363_13.htm.

16 David Robinson, from *Urban Mission*, excerpted on the Urbana website, www.urbana.org.

17 Nicholl, Charles *Borderlines (Journey in Thailand and Burma)* (London: Secker & Warburg Ltd, 1988), p 181.

18 *The Economist* December 4 2003.

19 *Operation World*'s figures, including everyone vaguely attached to all the Christian churches in all their forms. If you count only members of Protestant churches, the figure is nearer 275,000. Thailand's population in mid-2004 is given by the *World Population Data Sheet* as 63.8m.

20 www.ecpat.net, article on Thailand, as at June 2004.

21 Alan Collingwood in WEC New Zealand's magazine *Worldwide*, August/Sept 2001.

22 Dave & Sandra Macmillan, interviewed in Chiang Mai in Aug 2002.

CHAPTER 3 CAMBODIA

23 I could not find a definitive casualty figure: perhaps there isn't one. If the figure for bombs is correct, however, it implies an extraordinary concentration of explosive power in a small area. Such power, falling unseen from distant B-52s, must have been utterly terrifying and destructive.

24 From a report by the Cambodian NGO

Project Against Domestic Violence, 2000.

25 *SAO Vision for Cambodia* 122 Summer 2003, p 11.

26 Ian Brown *Cambodia* (Oxfam GB, 2000), p 7.

27 From *Getting People thinking*: Ideas from Christian Outreach's ABCD programme, Cambodia.

28 These were the two leading responses to questions about serving the community in a survey of 257 Cambodian Church leaders in 2004.

29 I'm grateful to Glenn Miles of Tearfund for these examples.

30 2 Corinthians 11: 19-21, NIV.

31 The official church figures are from *Operation World*, 2001. One estimate of the unofficial numbers came from Bob Harvey, who published a report on Christianity in Vietnam for *The Ottawa Citizen*, April 29 2000. Based on conversations with 20 or so leading Vietnamese pastors, he estimated 3,500 unofficial congregations.

32 Pastor Lap Mu, quoted in Release International's brochure *Love in Action*, May 2003.

33 See for example, *Response* (the magazine of Christian Solidarity International), April 2001, p 2-3.

34 See the Open Doors *World Watch List*, January 2004.

CHAPTER 4 JAPAN

35 Curtis Andresson *A Short History of Japan* (Australia: Allen & Unwin, 2002), p 49.

36 Japan's Defence Forces have controversially been deployed in peace-keeping roles in Iraq, but that is about the complete extent of their overseas involvement in the past 60 years.

37 Interestingly, American commentators talk of the 9/11 attacks in much the same way.

38 Lisa Martineau *Caught in a Mirror: Reflections of Japan* (London: Macmillan, 1993), p 27.

39 For example, a gospel of Matthew in old Chinese script was found inside the Koryuji Buddhist Temple in Kyoto. A Persian Christian physician named Rimitsu is believed to have served the Japanese Emperor from around 724-748. The Empress Komyo was much influenced by him and built an orphanage, a hospital and a leprosarium. In the Tokyo National Museum, two beams of a seventh century temple have crosses inscribed in them. You can find these claims in the online book, by John M L Young, of the Japan Presbyterian Mission *By Foot to China, the mission of the church of the East to 1400*, on the website of the Assyrian International News Agency www.aina.org/books/bftc/bftc.pdf.

40 Though actually he got his RSI in India, not Japan.

41 Of course, that is exactly how Christianity initially spread through Europe.

42 Sadly their faith appears to have severely decayed during the long wait, and had accumulated Shinto-like elements.

43 Jack Seward, *The Japanese* (Chicago: Passport Books, 1992) p 200.

44 Mari Umehara, quoted on the website www.jcfn.org.

45 Missionary Eric Kurfman referred me to the book *Human relations in a vertical society* by Chie Nakane. A number of her books on Japanese society are available in English translation.

46 See for example, www.simplechurch.org.uk.

47 Martineau, p 207.

FOR PRAYER

MYANMAR, THAILAND & CAMBODIA

1. Pray for the Church to grow and the gospel to spread among the majority peoples of the region, the Burman, the Thai and the Khmer. Except among the Khmer, churches are small and growth is slow.

2. Give thanks for the way many of the minority tribal peoples throughout the region have embraced the gospel. Pray for the evangelization of all the smaller peoples. Pray for the tribal churches. As we have seen, some bear a wonderful witness; others are highly compromised or nominal in their faith. Pray for peace and justice in the tribal conflicts in the region.

3. Pray that the gospel will thrive in the face of ancient spirit-worshipping traditions and modern materialism. Pray that the Christian community will grow in confidence and effectively challenge these two forms of idolatry.

4. Pray for just and good governments in the whole region. Pray that the churches will be salt and light to the communities around them.

JAPAN

1. Thank God for the churches and Christian workers who are serving in Japan.

2. Pray for a new day for the Christian faith in Japan: new thinking, new energy, fresh growth, a new movement of the Holy Spirit

3. Pray for the many students and tourists who travel out of Japan. Give thanks for the way that a number have responded to the gospel. Pray that they will be able to strengthen the Church in Japan when they return.